Hallelujah!

Recording chapels and meeting houses

1985

Council for British Archaeology

Published 1985 by the Council for British Archaeology, 112 Kennington Road, London SE11 6RE

British Library Cataloguing in Publication Data

Hallelujah! : recording chapels and meeting houses.
1. Church architecture—Great Britain—History
2. Chapels—Great Britain—History
I. Council for British Archaeology
726'.5'0941 NA5461

ISBN 0-906780-49-7

Produced by computer-controlled phototypesetting and printed offset
by UNWIN BROTHERS LTD., The Gresham Press, Old Woking, Surrey.
A member of the Martins Printing Group.

Contents

This booklet has been compiled jointly by members of the Nonconformist Working Party of the Council for British Archaeology. The principal contributors were Mr H Godwin Arnold (chapter 1), Mr Roger Thorne (chapters 2, 4), Mr David Butler (chapter 3), and Mr George McHardy (chapter 5), with considerable editorial revision by Mr Christopher Stell and further assistance from Dr Clyde Binfield. The respective authors or editors are alone responsible for any opinions expressed.

List of illustrations

Introduction

The principal object of this booklet is to draw attention to the part which individuals and local societies can play in the study and recording of a much neglected part of our national architectural heritage. Ecclesiastical buildings have long been respected as providing some of the best and most refined examples of the art of architecture. Antiquary and holidaymaker alike have directed their steps to the parish church in the assurance that the door would be open and that, even in the most modest of places, some object of interest would be found to stimulate the enquiring mind. Today many of these doors are closed and the erstwhile visitor must run the gauntlet of wrong addresses, absent ministers, and the unending vagaries of keyholders before reaching, if not abandoning, the chosen goal. To students of nonconformist architecture these problems are not new: accustomed to finding the wicket gate closed and barred they may well cry Hallelujah! on discovering it open.

But what do we see in these places? How do they compare with what are usually thought of as 'churches'? And, indeed, are they churches at all? — for the oldest are, at least historically, 'meeting houses', buildings to give shelter rather than to inspire awe. To these and many other questions some answers have been attempted, but as 'beauty lies in the eye of the beholder' so does appreciation of nonconformist architecture lie in our willingness to understand its purpose and limitations. A simple meeting house is no less charming for its simplicity, and a grand town chapel is not to be despised for the grandeur of its fittings, even though the ascetic may add, in the words of John Wesley, 'How can the old coarse gospel find admission here?'

Varieties of style, date, and denomination may leave the researcher bewildered by the richness of the field into which he has stumbled. But it is a transient glory and much urgent work is required both in recording and in education if the continued erosion of our limited resources of chapels and meeting houses is to be stemmed. No nonconformist chapel, however great and apparently respected, can be assumed to be safe from the prospect of unwarranted alteration or the threat of untimely demolition. Never was there a greater need to take stock of those that remain or for that eternal vigilance which is the price of liberty.

1 The historical and architectural background

> The Lord said to Moses: 'Tell the Israelites to make an offering to me. Receive whatever offerings any man wishes to give.... The people must make a sacred tent so that I may live among them. Make it and all its furnishings according to the plan that I will show you.'
> Exodus, xv, 1–2, 9, *Good News Bible*

> Look that thou make *them* after their pattern, which was shewed thee in the mount.
> *ibid*, xv, 40 *(AV)*

Christian architecture may be seen as making a place where the Lord may live among his people, and the differences from one denomination to another as so many different descriptions of the pattern which men have perceived 'in the mount'. Among these descriptions there are two extremes, the one of glory, the other of simplicity. Each has theological and scriptural justification. For the best exposition of the first one can look to Eusebius's *History of the Church* which concludes with the sermon delivered on the occasion of the dedication of the cathedral of Tyre, rebuilt in the time of the Emperor Constantine I after its destruction in time of persecution. The building is extensive, elaborate, rich, and ornamented; its parts, its elements, the act of its rebuilding, the building itself, are all made to symbolize images which reflect and illuminate each other — depicting the glories of heaven, and Christ's restoration of the ruined human soul.

For the other extreme there is the Quaker George Fox's terse 'Christ's people are his temple'. The fellowship of his church is to be the true image of his glory and the place where his spirit is to live. The building is to be but the simplest setting for that life.

If these two represent the opposite ends of a scale, then the medieval cathedrals and great churches stood close to one end. At the Reformation the scale was cut short; images were destroyed as superstitious and pictures and paintings were whitewashed over. Although in the early Middle Ages there are records of the wealthy hauling stone like labourers in the same spirit as 19th century artisans gave their skills to building Zion, the more elaborate the structure the costlier it was. Increasingly, therefore, and above all in the case of the great rebuilding of St Peter's in Rome, their financing involved all manner of expedients, the selling of indulgences the most notorious among them.

The need to purify the Christian church cried out to Dante two and a half centuries before the Reformation. When that came the Lutheran reformation was the more moderate in its rejection of forms and usages from the past, the Calvinist was the more destructive. A third group,

Fig 1 Bramhope, West Yorkshire: Puritan chapel, 1649 (photo: R Morris)

which found that reform of faith had not brought reform of manners, aimed at Primitive Christianity revived. All therefore cut short the scale to a greater or lesser degree, and nonconformist buildings, particularly in an English Protestant setting, can be expected to tend toward this opposite end of the scale.

Before considering differences between the buildings of one denomination and another it is as well to look first at the common ground. The starting date for nonconformist architecture can be taken as the Civil War (Fig 1), which can also be taken as the dividing line in building between 'medieval survival' and 'Gothic revival'. During the 17th and 18th centuries and much of the 19th century the dominant architectural style was the classical, first seriously represented in England by the work of Inigo Jones as royal architect. Gothic was a term of denigration; the styles and the ideas of the Middle Ages were regarded as barbarous compared with the enlightenment of ancient Rome revived. On the other hand, since most building was done without the employment of a professional designer, old traditions continued long and changed but slowly. So while a minority of Anglican churches in the 18th century had classical temple-style porticoes, most still had towers or steeples. The meeting houses of dissenters were recognizably similar to houses and cottages in the vernacular traditions of building (Fig 2).

If domestic buildings provide one element in the ancestry of noncon-

Fig 2 Tewkesbury, Gloucestershire: medieval timber-framed house converted to Baptist meeting house in 17th century (photo: NMR, Crown copyright reserved)

formist design, two others are provided by Wren's rebuilding of City of London churches after the Great Fire and by Continental Reformed buildings. In the Church of England after the Reformation medieval buildings with their many subdivisions and screened chancels were not well adapted for a form of worship which placed great emphasis on all the congregation being able to see and hear clearly all that was said and acted. An early way of dealing with the problem was to bring the communion table away from the old position of the altar at the east wall, but this was emphatically rejected by Archbishop Laud. The next alternative was to use the building as if it were two rooms. The chancel, with the table in its old place and its stalls if any, became the place to which the congregation withdrew for communion. The body of the church then served as the setting for all other worship. With the sermon forming a prominent part of the service the pulpit became an important feature. With large congregations leading to the introduction of galleries for extra seating a raised pulpit became essential, and so the 'three-decker' was evolved. Using the lowest desk was the parish clerk, who was both a civil officer and the leader of the congregation, a reading pew was on the middle level, and the pulpit at the third. Frequently this assemblage would be placed in the central aisle, at the entrance to the chancel, and so it appears in many an old engraving of unaltered churches. The restoration of such churches in Victorian times entirely changed and removed these arrangements, and their rearrangements are often now being in turn replaced by resiting the table at the head of the nave and removing the choir stalls.

In rebuilding after the Great Fire, Sir Christopher Wren was able to avoid these inconveniences of adaptation and to design from first principles. Galleries were accepted to bring numbers within easy hearing, but long chancels, being unnecessary, were avoided and only the shallowest recess, if any, was provided. Choir stalls were not made for robed choirs and were not seen in parish churches until the 19th century, and church organs were comparatively rare also. If there was an organ it would be in the west gallery, together with the singers, and this also would be the place for the band of instruments or church orchestra. St James's Church in Piccadilly was a clear expression of Wren's practical skill and architectural principles, and of contemporary Anglican attitudes and observances. As such it provided a precedent followed for nearly 200 years. The typical Anglican church new-built in the 17th or 18th century would therefore usually be rectangular in shape with galleries on three sides. The roof and galleries would be supported on stone or timber columns of one of the classical orders. A panelled reredos and a railed enclosure to the holy table distinguished the sanctuary. In the largest churches the pulpit would be in the central position as described (Fig 3); in others it might be placed to one side.

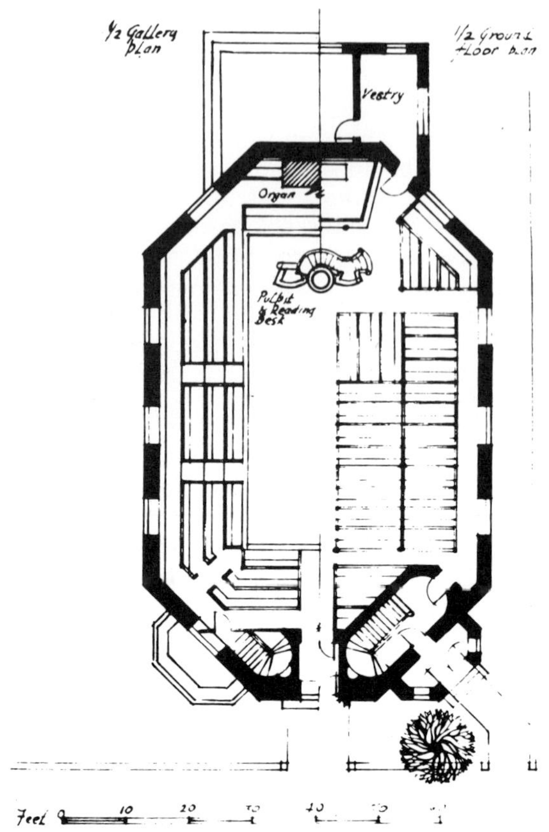

Fig 3 Chichester, West Sussex: church of St John, 1812–13 (plan: H Godwin Arnold)

Continental Reformed buildings perhaps provide nearer precedents, as might be expected, for Protestant nonconformist buildings. In common with the churches just mentioned they generally kept the rectangular galleried form but differed in their liturgical arrangements. Free of the feeling that the only place for the table was against a wall it could, in a manner much more expressive of the unity between the Last Supper and the sacrament, be set near or among the assembly of the people. The pulpit, from which the minister presided, could then sensibly be placed against the wall. Reformed church buildings in Amsterdam and elsewhere on the Continent, and above all the great French Protestant 'Temple' at Charenton, were patterns (Fig 4).

In attempting to summarize the different characteristics of the buildings of several denominations over a period it must be allowed that generaliz-

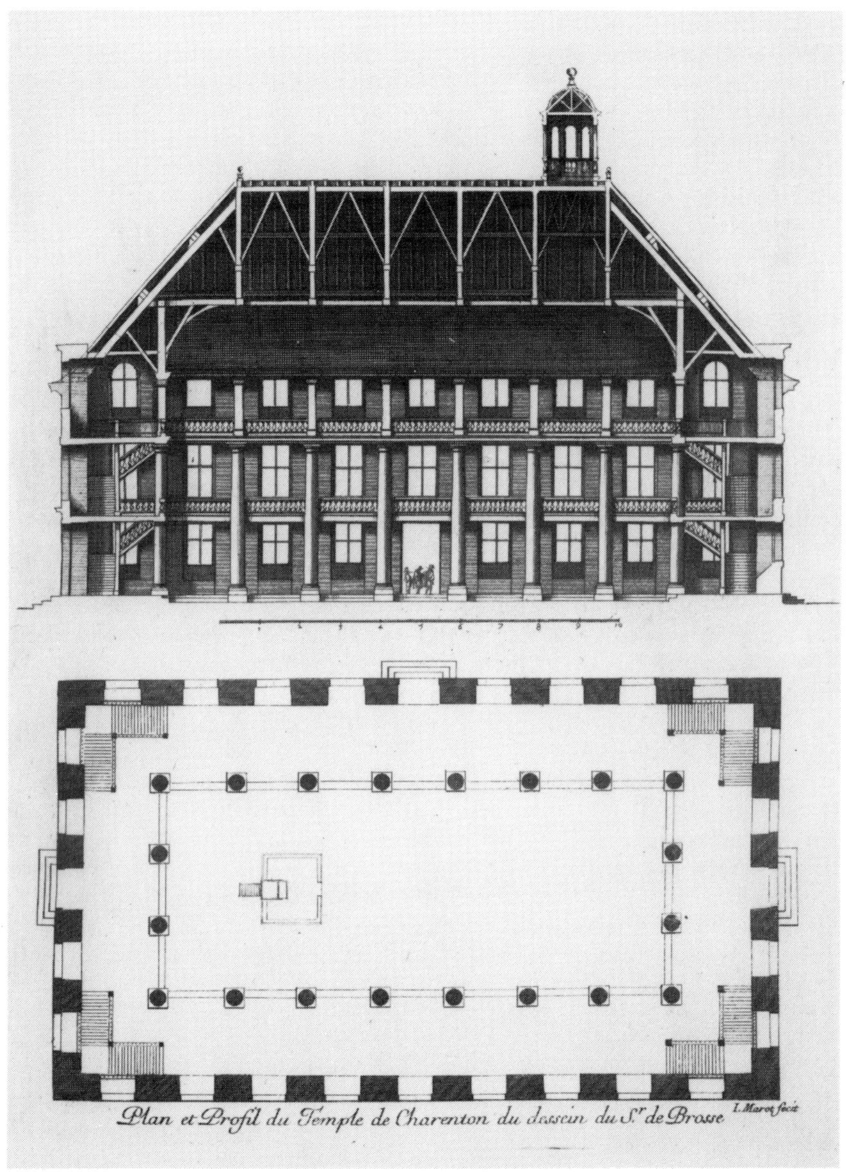

Fig 4 Charenton: section and plan of Protestant temple (plan and section, Grand Marot: RIBA)

ations must be clumsy and cannot be exact over centuries at all times and in all instances. If, again, one sets out two extremes there is at one end a small and humble meeting house in a remote dale seating perhaps 100 people on backless benches, with a stable opposite for the horses of those who had ridden from a distance, and at the other the chapel of a prosperous Victorian congregation in an industrial town, seating upwards of 1000 'under' a popular preacher together with its Sunday School rooms, library, and minister's house. In inner city areas these are now commonly as much of a problem as the excess of small medieval parish churches in an historic town, but, like those — 'when your children and your grandchildren say to you "what is the meaning of these stones?" ' — they also tell of the people of the past and of their work.

Within the immense range it is, however, possible to make some distinctions. There are those of circumstances and those which reflect differences of theology, of emphasis, of church order, and administration of sacraments. Two elementary distinctions of circumstance are the presence or absence of persecution or legal proscription, and the distinction of wealth or poverty. Until the Toleration Act of 1689 those worshipping in 'conventicles' apart from the Established church were liable to severe penalties. Nonetheless, a substantial number of Quaker meeting houses dated from before 1670, with others set up in the period up to 1682 when a renewed outbreak of persecution caused building to cease until 1686. Buildings of this early period, which owed their survival to the tolerance of the local justices or to their remoteness, tended also therefore to be relatively plain and simple, although the fine early Friends' meeting houses at Hertford (1670) and Briggflatts near Sedbergh (1675) are in their way quite substantial. Similarly, before the Catholic Relief Act of 1778 by which, among other penalties, that of lifelong imprisonment for keeping a Catholic school was abolished, Catholic chapels (apart from those of foreign embassies and the private chapels of Catholic families) were plain and discreet, outwardly resembling perhaps a stable or workshop, where rather than 'going to Mass' their adherents spoke cautiously of 'prayers'. Even in 1789 the private chapel at Mapledurham House in Oxfordshire (Fig 5) was apparently built to resemble an extension of the servants' quarters. Freedom from persecution combined with prosperity enabled buildings to be as lavish as the principles and the prosperity of the patron or congregation chose.

There is a high degree of simplicity in the buildings (Fig 6) and mode of worship of the Society of Friends, which owes its first inspiration to the work of George Fox; much of its organization is still as he shaped it. He started preaching in 1647 at the age of 23 and in the next year formed his earliest settled congregation at Mansfield. The year 1652 brought a significant increase with the addition of large numbers of the 'Seekers' of Westmorland, who had been in the habit of worshipping together in silence

Fig 5 Mapledurham House, Oxfordshire: private chapel of Roman Catholic family (photo: NMR, Crown copyright reserved)

Fig 6 Hertford: Friends' meeting house, 1670; interior prior to repair in 1981 (photo: NMR, Crown copyright reserved)

apart from all other churches and sects in hope for the coming of new apostles. Numbers reached a peak early in the 18th century, but emigration to America, estimated at 500 members a year during the last quarter of the 17th century, and a retreat from the early missionary zeal which defied all persecution, left numbers steady, many a country meeting being sustained by a few faithful families. The practice of disownment for such various offences against discipline as bankruptcy and 'marrying out' was not abandoned until the second half of the 19th century after it had done much damage. Twentieth century numbers in Britain are perhaps half those of the 17th century. Prime among virtues Quakers place faithfulness and obedience to truth and the light of Christ. This is expressed in such observances as meeting for worship on the basis of silence, the conduct of business without voting, and scrupulous honesty.

The Baptist churches trace their origin to the work of John Smyth, a Separatist exile in Amsterdam who in 1609 reinstituted the baptism of adult believers as the foundation of church membership. They were pioneers in the plea for freedom of conscience and religious liberty. From an early date two distinct Baptist groups emerged, the General Baptists with an Arminian theology and the Particular Baptists who formed the majority and were strongly Calvinistic in their outlook. A regrouping in the late 18th century and after as their theological positions began to merge saw the rise of a High Calvinist wing of Strict Baptists while the older General Baptists in the south of England found a greater community of interest with the Unitarians. Orthodox Baptists attach great importance to the New Testament in regulating church order and practice, and for this reason have from the mid 17th century practised baptism by immersion or 'dipping' instead of by affusion or sprinkling. In early days baptism took place in ponds or streams (Fig 7), but internal baptisteries are now provided in most chapels. Prayer book services were viewed with suspicion: in the words of John Smyth the use of service books was 'the invention of the man of sin' and was incompatible with the spiritual worship shown in the New Testament, proceeding from the heart. In the 17th century even the singing of hymns was a matter for heated debate. In organization these churches belong in the tradition of congregational independence, maintaining the 'crown rights of the Redeemer', the headship of Christ over each congregation. As with the Congregationalists, the theoretical isolation of each unit is in practice taken up into the fellowship of County and National Unions.

As early as 1550 there is evidence of congregations meeting together to hear the Word of God and to receive the sacraments apart from the Church of England; when it became clear that Queen Elizabeth did not intend the changes they looked for their number increased. These Separatists, 'gathered churches' as distinct from the national or 'multitudinous' church established by law, are the origin of Independency or

Fig 7 Rode, Somerset: public baptism (lithograph: W W Wheatley (NMR))

Congregationalism, a movement which is now largely contained within the United Reformed Church. An early influence was the teaching of Robert Browne, who at one stage emigrated with his Norwich congregation to Middleburg in Holland. Independents were persecuted in Stuart times and by their emigration to the American colonies did much to shape the religion and the politics of what is now the United States. They were prominent in Cromwell's army and in the political and religious debates of the Civil War and Commonwealth period. The association of their churches in the Congregational Union of England and Wales dates from 1832 but, while designed to help and advise its member churches, this had no power to legislate over them. The United Reformed Church, which was formed in 1972, unites two traditions that in origin and in theory were altogether distinct, with Presbyterianism collegial, and indeed tending to the hierarchical in structure, and Congregationalism or Independency democratic. The Presbyterians, as descendants of the Calvinist Reformation, have never shared the reservations which the churches of the Radical Reformation have concerning the power of the state to coerce,.punish, and make war. Attempts at union in the 17th century failed mainly because, although both were generally Calvinist, the Congregationalists were per-

Fig 8 Dukinfield, Greater Manchester (Cheshire): Old Chapel, a rebuilding of 1840 (photo: NMR, Crown copyright reserved)

force more tolerant, and also more evangelical in attitude. Of the two the Independents were, from the start, the nearer to the churches so far described, with emphases both biblical and charismatic. John Owen, the Puritan vice-chancellor of Oxford, accused the imposers of liturgies of bringing persecution into the church — bringing 'fire and faggot into the Christian religion'. It is indeed at this point that we cross a divide. For these Independents, as for Fox, the imposition of set forms of worship, under penalties legislated by 'the higher power' in St Paul's phrase, and changed with each change in the state religion — mass, common prayer, mass restored, common prayer, directory — was not the work of Christians.

The history of the Presbyterians as a denomination is chequered; from a high peak, when they had a majority in the Westminster Assembly of Divines appointed in 1643 by the Long Parliament to reform the doctrine and worship of the Church of England in a Puritan direction, their influence, though not their 'respectability', declined catastrophically in the century following. By the end of the 18th century, while some Presbyterian congregations had become effectively Independent in organization, merging into Congregationalism, many others, together with some General Baptists, had adopted those Arian or Unitarian views of which more hereafter. A further group of Presbyterian churches, largely Scottish in origin or ministry, and reorganized in 1876 as the Presbyterian Church of England, is the other major partner in the United Reformed Church. An essential Presbyterian principle is of a governing hierarchy starting at the first level with the minister and elders of the particular congregation, and ascending through the presbytery of similar representatives of a district, the synod of a larger area, and finally the General Assembly. Some Presbyterians use a liturgy and others avoid set forms. The original Calvinist rite involved the congregation coming forward to the table to receive communion standing. The service was conducted from the table, with readings and sermon from the pulpit. Only later, under the influence of a very high reverence for the Lord's Supper which made the taking of communion infrequent, did the centre of emphasis gravitate to the pulpit. The importance of preaching was greatly stressed by Calvin and John Knox, and its position in the life of the church is marked by the prominence given to the pulpit.

Like others of the distinctive beliefs referred to, Unitarianism lays claim to a long ancestry, although its established communities do not appear before the Reformation. Early groups are found in Poland and in Hungary. In England the writings of John Biddle led to short-lived conventicles in the metropolis in 1652–4 and 1657–62, but not until 1774, when Theophilus Lindsay opened Essex Chapel in London, was an overtly Unitarian congregation formally established. Preaching contrary to the doctrine of the Trinity remained illegal until the passing of the Trinity Act in 1813. Many of their older churches originated with the ejection in 1662 of those ministers who could not subscribe to the Act of Uniformity. Some 2000 refused to conform and by continuing to preach brought about the formation of many originally orthodox dissenting congregations, then generally described as Presbyterian. Exclusion of nonconformists from the Universities of Oxford and Cambridge, a disability which was not finally removed until 1871, made essential the establishment of the Dissenting Academies, institutions which catered for the training of an educated ministry. The Academies, although of great importance in the history of education in this country, not infrequently moved with the ministers who conducted them and so have left few buildings which still survive in recognizable form. As institutions they are now represented by such colleges as Manchester College at Oxford, or the Baptist College in Bristol. Joseph Priestley, who trained at the Academy at Daventry, and in 1761 became tutor at that established at Warrington, was noted as a scientist and was one of the founders of the Unitarian Society in 1791. It is due to a continuity of ownership rather than a continuity of belief that a high proportion of Unitarian chapels are those on sites originally built upon by orthodox Presbyterians. As compared with most of the early Quaker and Baptist meeting houses they are larger, more stately, and ornate (Fig 8). Their congregations represented the aristocracy of dissent with whom the

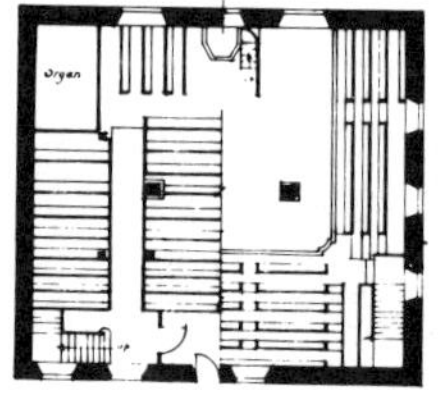

Fig 9 Taunton, Somerset: Mary Street chapel, 1721 (drawing and plan: H Godwin Arnold)

enthusiasm of lesser sects was anathema and where the scholarly logic of *avant garde* ministers fresh from the academies found ready acceptance. In this respect the formerly Baptist chapel in Mary Street, Taunton (Fig 9), is a notable exception.

The gradual change in belief led not only to the setting up of rival orthodox congregations but also to much-contested ownership of the buildings, which was only settled by the passing of the Dissenters Chapels Act in 1844.

Another church with ancient roots on the Continent is that of the Moravian or United Brethren. These originated with the followers of John Hus, martyred in 1415, and were organized as a distinct episcopal church

Fig 10   Fulneck, West Yorkshire: portion of Moravian settlement (photo: R Morris)

Fig 11a Norwich: octagon, 1754–56 (lithograph of 1848 in J & D Taylor, History of the Octagon Chapel, Norwich: NMR, Crown copyright reserved)

in 1457, then meeting at Kunwald on the borders of Silesia and Moravia. Persecution and exile made their survival precarious until, in 1721, they joined with others on the estate of Count Zinzendorf at Herrnhut in Saxony. The year 1727 is generally taken as the date of the reconstitution of the Moravian Church. Education and missionary work are particularly strong in their tradition, and the 'settlement', a community with its own group of buildings comprising chapel, schools, and separate houses for the various groups called 'choirs' (boys, girls, brethren, and sisters), was the ideal form of their establishment. John Wesley's visit to the colony at Herrnhut had a profound effect on his own religious life. The number of Moravian congregations in England is small but in the context of nonconformist architecture they are important because of this characteristic wish to build, figuratively speaking, a close community of the faithful, and hence literally to build self-contained groups of buildings which are without parallel in other denominations (Fig 10).

Presbyterians, Independents, Baptists, and Quakers together made up what has been called the 'Old Dissent'. The 'New Dissent', dating from the mid 18th century, was the result of a religious revival centred largely on the work of the Wesleys and their Methodist societies, reluctant though

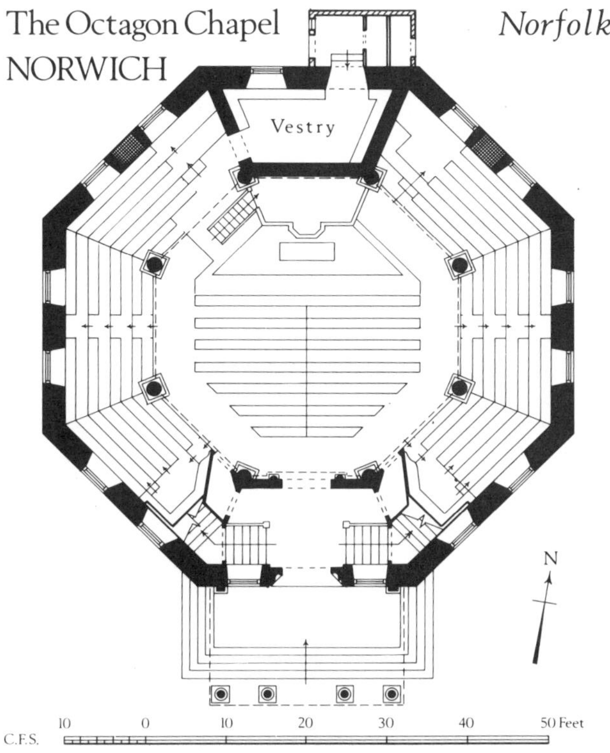

Fig 11b Norwich: octagon (plan: C F Stell, Crown copyright reserved)

they were at first to accept such a designation.

The background of Methodism is different from that of the denominations so far considered. John Wesley began his field preaching at Kingswood in 1739 but as an ordained minister of the Established church he had no intention of separation; his aim was to 'promote vital practical religion and by the grace of God to beget, preserve, and increase the life of God in the souls of men.' His wish was for his followers to remain within the Church of England. By the time of his death these numbered over 100,000 in Britain and America. Anxious always to avoid the appearance of dissent, he particularly objected to the necessity of registering his chapels as dissenters' meeting houses. In intention Wesley's 'societies' were to be complementary to the activity of Anglican parishes, and accordingly their work centred on class and fellowship meetings and midweek preaching services. Gradually separation was forced by the unwelcoming attitude of clergy and active persecution by Anglican laymen. There is therefore an evolution in Methodist buildings in accord with their purposes in that the earliest made no provision for the celebration of Holy Communion. At the next stage their function had sufficient similarities to that of dissenting meeting houses for these to provide a natural precedent. Indeed, Wesley was so enamoured of the Presbyterian octagon chapel in Norwich (Fig 11) that he recommended the plan for his own chapels, some fourteen of which were built in this form. By contrast, Wesley's City Road chapel in London of 1778 was very similar in arrangement to Wren's church of St James, Piccadilly, and both can be seen as originally clearly expressing in architectural terms the basic tenets of Protestantism — a single hall with no marked separation between nave and chancel, and a central pulpit with a communion area behind.

If conformity or otherwise to the Established church is to be our sole criterion, the Roman Catholic Church may also be termed 'nonconformist', though of a different kind. Its early churches and houses of the post-Reformation period closely resemble in many ways those of Protestant dissent. There is the same use of a generally classical vernacular style and, from a comparable need to secure safety by obscurity, the same lack of architectural display.

James II's Declaration of Indulgence of 1687, ostensibly with the object of granting religious freedom to all, made clear that Quaker Meetings and Mass could alike go unpunished, even though the Penal Laws and the Conventicle Acts remained unrepealed. Although regarded with suspicion by the majority of nonconformists and soon overturned by the subsequent revolution, this respite permitted the erection of a handful of new buildings, but for the greater part of the 18th century Catholic chapels were few in number, discreet and simple, concealed in back alleys, or close to the house of a Catholic family; most were still only a room in a mansion or farmhouse. There was the risk of destruction by soldiery at least until 1716, and by town mobs as late as 1780, in which year, for example, the newly-built Catholic chapel in Bath, largely subscribed for by families who visited the spa, was gutted two days before the first Mass was to be held. The Relief Act of 1791 at last legalized the building of Catholic chapels for public worship. In Lancashire, a county where Catholicism remained comparatively strong, buildings remain from this period; they may even have been put up by the same builders who erected chapels for other denominations, for their outward form is very similar. Inwardly, the similarity is more with contemporary Anglican buildings: simple rectangular structures with galleries and shallow chancels and an altar backed by a panelled reredos in classical style. Where the Anglican reredos would by law have the two tables of the Commandments, generally flanked by the Creed and the Lord's Prayer, the Catholic would by custom commonly have a religious painting such as the crucifixion, resurrection, or ascension. The prominent pulpit of contemporary Protestant buildings will, however, never be found. The manner of worship is wholly liturgical and, while preaching and

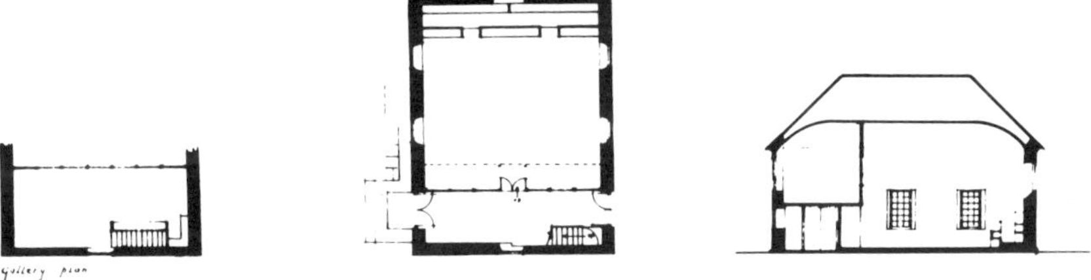

Fig 12 Long Sutton, Somerset: Friends' meeting house, 1717 (watercolour: H Godwin Arnold)

teaching have their place, the emphasis is very different and the buildings differ accordingly.

Quaker meeting houses have nearly as wide a range of size as the buildings of any of the other denominations. The smallest are single rooms, smaller even than most cottages, and built in the local vernacular manner. At the other extreme, in some large towns, there are complexes which incorporate a large and a small meeting house, library and committee rooms, and perhaps a caretaker's house. Intermediate in size, but not in form, is that illustrated (Fig 12) at Long Sutton in Somerset, which has a degree of architectural presence more usual in a substantial town, and in form and details is influenced by the Renaissance style of Wren. This is a rectangle some 35ft by 47ft, built in local stones, a good tawny limestone for details combined with a softer blue-grey lias. The hipped

Fig 13 Reading, Berkshire: Baptist chapel, 1860 (photo: NMR, Crown copyright reserved)

roof is covered with West Country slates above two courses of stone tiles, a common detail in Wessex, and it has a wooden classical cornice at the eaves. The date of the building is 1717. A wealthy Quaker, William Steele, gave a piece of orchard opposite the early meeting house with £200 for a new building on condition that Friends hauled the materials. His gift is commemorated by a small tablet above one of the windows inscribed 'Ex Dono/Willmi Steell/Anno Dom/1717'. On each long side are two windows and a doorway. The doorways have wide segmental hoods and lead into a stone-floored lobby divided from the main room by a partition with panels which can be opened. Above this, and reached by a single staircase from the lobby, is a wider gallery similarly divided from the meeting house. At the opposite end of the room, which has a single central window, there is what is known as the 'stand', or the ministers' gallery, two tiers of fixed seating with panelled backs. Facing these are two rows of long benches, having shaped arm-rests and railed, open backs. The only other furniture is a table in front of the stand on which a Bible is normally placed but which in business meetings is used for the Clerk's papers and minute book.

The surrounding graveyard has lines of largely identical gravestones. Monuments to the dead were strongly disapproved of by Quakers between 1715 and 1850 and most earlier stones were removed, but stones of a simple uniform design were later permitted. In this, as in the absence of any form of carving, decoration, or ornament on the building and in the use of unstained and unpolished wood, the Quaker testimony for plainness and against extravagant display is evident.

The successive moves of the Baptist Church in Reading can be taken as reasonably representative of that denomination (Fig 13). The date stone on the chapel in King's Road records:

> Founded in Church Street 1640 Removed to Hosier Street 1752
> And to this spot 1834 Enlarged 1858 Further enlarged 1860

The first meeting house was in a small street almost in the shadow of one of Reading's three ancient parish churches which is dedicated to St Giles, the patron saint of travellers, and stood therefore at what was for some centuries the very edge of the town. Hosier Street was more central, and King's Road a new-made thoroughfare when the county town began to expand eastward toward London with handsome stone-built villas. The architect of the 1834 building was John James Cooper, architect and builder (as was not uncommon at the period), Surveyor to the Paving Commissioners of Reading, and Treasurer of the Borough Fund. For at least three generations the Cooper family was attached to the King's Road church. Loyalty to the professionals of own's own denomination and church was general in the 19th century and conversely tended to prevent them working for other bodies. As a High Church architect, William Butterfield was reticent about his early works for nonconformists. The selection of A W N Pugin as architect for an Anglican church, school, and rectory at Tubney near Oxford in 1845 is unusual on both counts. Methodists usually went to Methodist architects, Congregationalists preferred architects of their own persuasion, and so on.

The frontage to King's Road of 1858–60 is in five bays with pilasters of the Doric order on pedestals and carrying a full entablature and pediment. Three doorways in the central bays have arched heads and fanlights. The upper tier of windows indicates the existence of a gallery. The facade is in good Bath stone with fine joints. The side walls are in ashlar of much inferior quality and workmanship. The roof is of Welsh slate, which had begun to reach Berkshire with the opening of the Oxford Canal late in the 18th century. The detail of the elevation is Italian Renaissance in style, with the somewhat unscholarly flavour typical of Victorian nonconformity.

The interior, under threat of demolition following a further move to a new building close at hand, is entirely typical of the substantial urban Free Church building of the 19th century. The plan is a rectangle with galleries around three sides entered by a pair of staircases symmetrically placed in the corners nearest the street; a separate gallery holds seats for a choir and a large organ, facing the congregation, behind and above the

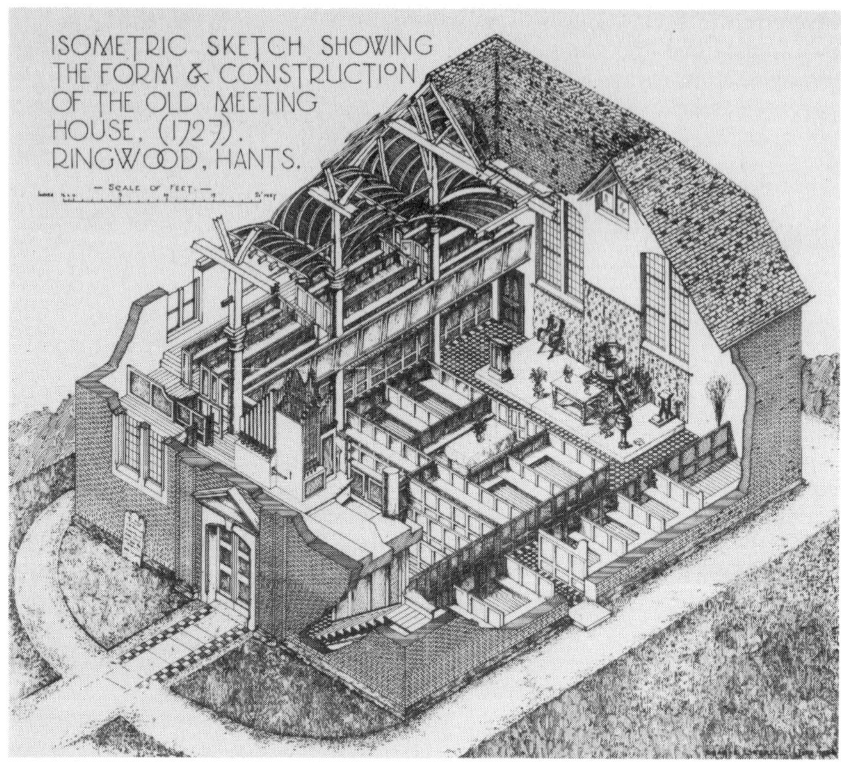

Fig 14 Ringwood, Hampshire: meeting house, 1727 (drawing: C E Linskill)

pulpit. The pulpit stands high, to command the galleries. Below and in front of it is a platform with communion table, six chairs for deacons, and a surrounding rail. Such interiors are so much to a standard pattern that it is quite usual to find that chapel buildings have passed from one denomination to another without need for any alteration. The only additional requirement in the case of the Baptists was a baptistery for total immersion, usually concealed below the platform.

An excellent example of an early Presbyterian meeting house, latterly Unitarian, now disused and closed, is the Old Meeting House at Ringwood in Hampshire, built in 1727 (Fig 14). The congregation originated with the ejection in 1662 of the Rev Compton South from the living of Berwick St John in Wiltshire and was under the patronage of Lady Lisle of Moyles Court, who died in Judge Jeffreys' 'Bloody Assize'. It was under her grandson, the Rev James Whitaker, that the meeting house was built.

This is a rectangular building of about 40ft by 50ft. The walls are of brick laid in English bond on the side walls and Flemish bond, an

Fig 15 Macclesfield, Cheshire: King Edward Street chapel, interior of 1690 (photo: NMR, Crown copyright reserved)

introduction of the late 17th century, only on the front. The roof is partly hipped as at Long Sutton, but lower eaves on the side walls give it a more barn-like character, less stylish architecturally than the other. The single door in the centre of the front has a pedimented stone surround.

The doorway leads into a lobby from which stairs rise to the gallery. The gallery follows three sides of the building. The central space has an arched plaster ceiling rising from two lines of tall timber columns, three on each side, which also support the galleries. Between the columns lesser arched ceilings run at right-angles to the main vault, the whole being based on the pattern of Wren's St James's Church, Piccadilly. The side galleries have rows of narrow pews; the cross-gallery has an organ which almost certainly could not have existed originally. Even in many Anglican churches, organs were unknown until the 19th century restorations and refurnishings, the singing being accompanied by the church orchestra, which as in Thomas Hardy's *Under the Greenwood Tree* could double as the village band or even serve church and chapel indiscriminately. On the front of the gallery is a large black and gilt laquered pendulum clock.

Unlike a medieval church, there is no central aisle; the central space is filled with pews approached from side aisles behind the main columns. Most of the ground floor pews are spacious enough to have a seat running

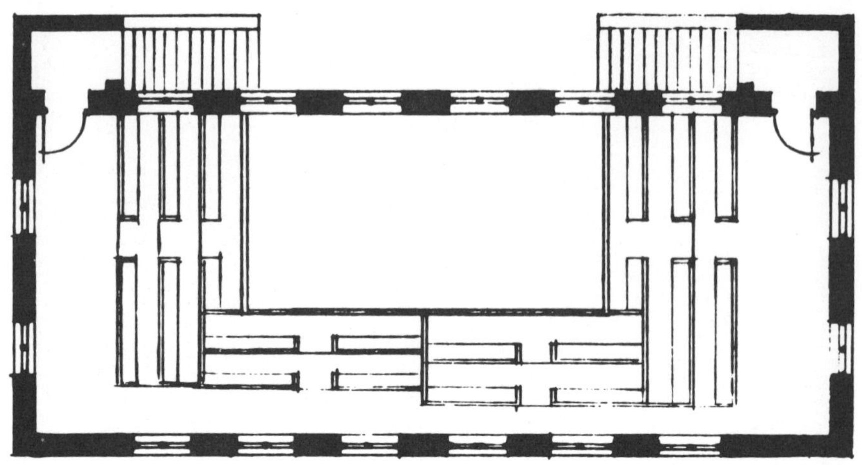

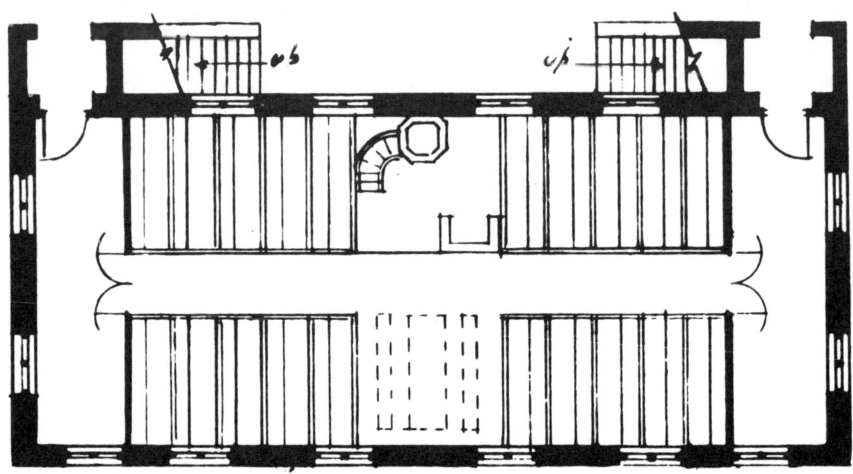

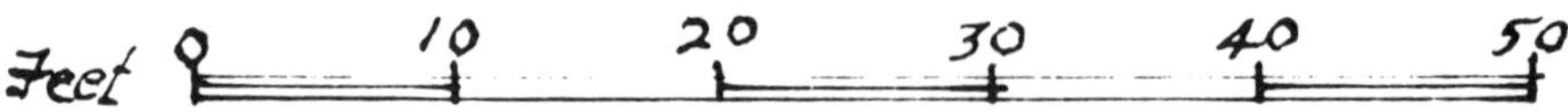

Fig 16 Knutsford, Cheshire: Brook Street chapel, c 1690 (plan: H Godwin Arnold)

Fig 17 Dean Row, Wilmslow, Cheshire: exterior of chapel, 1690s (photo: H Godwin Arnold)

round three sides of their enclosure. In the centre is a 'table pew' — a similar panelled enclosure with a seat surrounding a table for communion. On the same centre line is a smaller table standing immediately below the pulpit, here introduced in the mid 19th century at a time when traditional practices were being abandoned, when the high pulpit was lowered, and an attempt was made to rename the building 'St Thomas's Chapel'. On each side of the pulpit is a tall window; the side walls have upper and lower windows. This arrangement, which denotes the presence of galleries and demarcates the site of the pulpit, often remains as evidence of the original arrangement even after a drastic refitting. The pulpit and the font, which is close at hand, appear to be Victorian. The pulpit has lost the large sounding board which would have been normal; the carved wooden dove, symbol of the Holy Spirit, still exists.

Although the font is not contemporary with the building its placing is in accordance with the Reformed principle expressed in the Westminster *Directory of Public Worship* of 1645 as 'Nor is it to be administer'd in private places, or privately, but in the place of publick worship, and in the face of the congregation, where people may most conveniently see and hear.' This arrangement, whereby pulpit, font, communion table, and reading desk are all concentrated in one space, making a single liturgical centre, has long been characteristic of Free Churches. Under the influence of the Liturgical movement it has become common in new Roman Catholic church buildings and similarly in the reordering of numerous Anglican churches.

The manner in which the communion service is administered has an influence on plans which is not always obvious. Opinions, customs, and changes in this respect are too numerous and complex to be described here, but reference must be made to one custom, still observed in the Calvinist churches of the Netherlands, for the communion to be taken by the congregation seated on benches at long tables put up in the central space of the church, so expressing it as a common meal at which as many as possible sit down together; this used also to be the practice in Scottish Presbyterian churches. In some early Presbyterian or Independent meeting houses, such as what is now the Unitarian chapel at Knutsford, one of an interesting group of buildings in Cheshire (Figs 15–17), there is, facing the pulpit, a wide space in which a table and benches were placed. However, since it was not felt right that 'the Lord's board should be spread and none partake', the influence of this arrangement is not perceived if the table or tables are not in place. At Littlecote House in Wiltshire a Cromwellian private chapel has a wide square space between the pulpit and the pews paved in black and white stone, with at its centre a pattern like a compass rose or a star. This is clearly intended to be the setting for a small circular table and even to give it some symbolic importance, but when that table is folded down to half-moon shape and stood to one side the intention of the plan can be quite misunderstood, and it can be interpreted as solely a place for preaching.

A Methodist building which deserves description, because it is unique in preserving a plan which was once widely used, is the chapel at Newbury in Berkshire (Fig 18). This also illustrates 20th century problems in that that congregation is a town centre church with reduced numbers and the burden of expensive repairs (aggravated by the imposition of Value Added Tax on repairs to historic buildings) to a structure designed with less regard for simple reliable construction than could have been wished.

In the main street of Newbury, Northbrook Street, to the south of the river bridge,is the stately parish church, built about 1500. Then in turn came the Presbyterian (later Unitarian) Meeting House of 1697, the Congregational chapel rebuilt in 1822, and lastly the Wesleyan Methodist chapel of 1837. Two of these are now demolished and the future of this last has long been in question. John Wesley first preached in Newbury in 1740 and the present Methodist society can be dated from 1770. Their building is essentially a rectangular hall 40ft by 60ft with a gallery on all four sides, and a very shallow extension similar to Wren's plan for St James's, Piccadilly. The use on the exterior of the Gothic style was at the

Fig 18a Newbury, Berkshire: Methodist chapel, 1837 (photo: NMR, Crown copyright reserved)

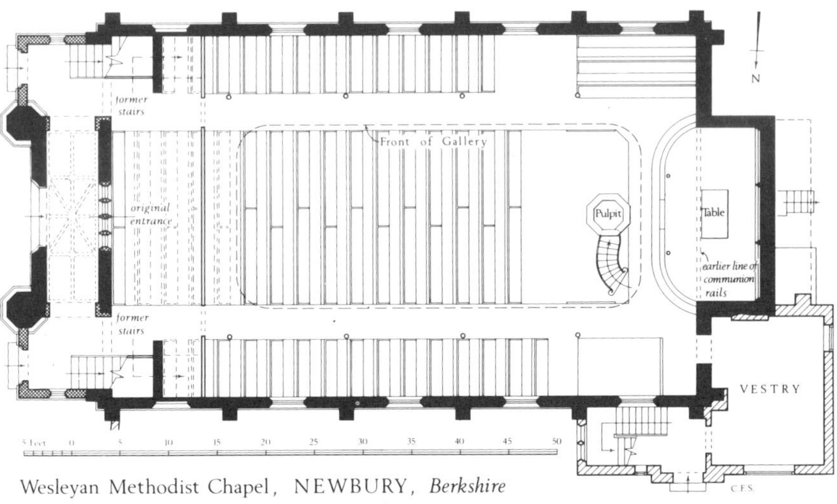

Fig 18b Newbury, Berkshire: Methodist chapel, 1837 (plan: C F Stell, Crown copyright reserved)

Fig 19 Newport, Isle of Wight: Pyle Street Methodist chapel, 1804, lengthened 1833 (photo: NMR, Crown copyright reserved)

time unusual for chapels and meeting houses; there was perhaps a tendency to distrust it as Romish, and the traditional Georgian exterior with arched windows and a low pitched roof was a rational design which there was little reason to abandon.

The unique feature of this building, which it still preserves, is an interior arrangement formerly common in Anglican churches and in Methodist chapels. This is for the pulpit, raised high on a slender pier to command the galleries, to stand directly in front of the communion table. Here the table stands in the alcove under the gallery and behind the pulpit. There is a communion rail around the shallow recess and its back wall has the Lord's Prayer, the two tables of the Commandments, and the Creed painted on panels with faintly Tudor Gothic frames. In Anglican chancels the Decalogue was required by Canon law (Canon LXXXII of 1604). The Creed and Lord's Prayer were not so ordered but were felt to be 'very fit companions' for the Commandments. All were certainly customary from the time of Wren until the middle of the 19th century.

As in other Protestant Nonconformist buildings, there being no require-

Fig 20 West Cowes, Isle of Wight: Roman Catholic church, 1796 (photo: NMR, Crown copyright reserved)

ment for a processional aisle, the centre of the floor is reasonably filled with pews, with the passages kept to the sides, close to the gallery pillars. The entrances have been altered to two from a former single central doorway, gallery stairs have been altered, and vestries and schoolrooms added.

The Methodist chapel in Pyle Street, Newport, in the Isle of Wight (Fig 19), built in 1804 and lengthened in 1833, was just such a rational Georgian brick box, but it had a different internal arrangement, with the pulpit raised as a rostrum filling a semicircular apse. The table was below and in front and surrounded by a semicircular rail. The elevation to the street has five arched windows, three at gallery level and one each side of a white Doric doorcase. Above is a brick gable formed as a pediment with a matching lunette window. It was closed about 1968 and has been converted to a theatre.

In the same street, but a generation earlier, is a Catholic church outwardly almost identical in form. This was the gift, with another at West Cowes (Fig 20), of Mrs Elizabeth Heneage, a wealthy convert, wife of a Catholic landlord in Lincolnshire. The chapel at Newport was registered in 1792, that at West Cowes in 1796. The two churches are

Fig 21 Cheadle, Staffordshire: Roman Catholic church, 1846, by A W N Pugin (photo: NMR, Crown copyright reserved)

Fig 22 Fulneck, West Yorkshire: interior of chapel of Moravian settlement, c 1742 (photo: NMR, Crown copyright reserved)

similarly rectangular and galleried on three sides. The Newport interior is the more simple, with only the minimum elaboration of the wall behind the altar by a very shallow arched apse forming an elliptical recess. The ends of the two aisles beneath the galleries are enclosed to form a sacristy on one side and a confessional on the other. Between them, on the line of the last pair of Ionic gallery columns, is the altar rail raised on a single step with another single step to the altar. The church at West Cowes has a far more elaborate altar composition occupying the whole end wall. The designer was the priest of the church, Father Thomas Gabb; and he created a design with a major round-arched recess framed by vigorous Roman Doric pilasters with architrave above and flanked by smaller arched recesses with statues on brackets. The whole has echoes of the style of Vanbrugh and Hawksmoor. The altar is of white and yellow marble. At this point one crosses a significant dividing line, that between stone altar and wooden table, of which the theological implications need not be elaborated.

These two neat and simple churches perfectly represent a stage in the evolution of Roman Catholic church building when it had, architecturally, scarcely separated itself from other denominations. Later, with increasing

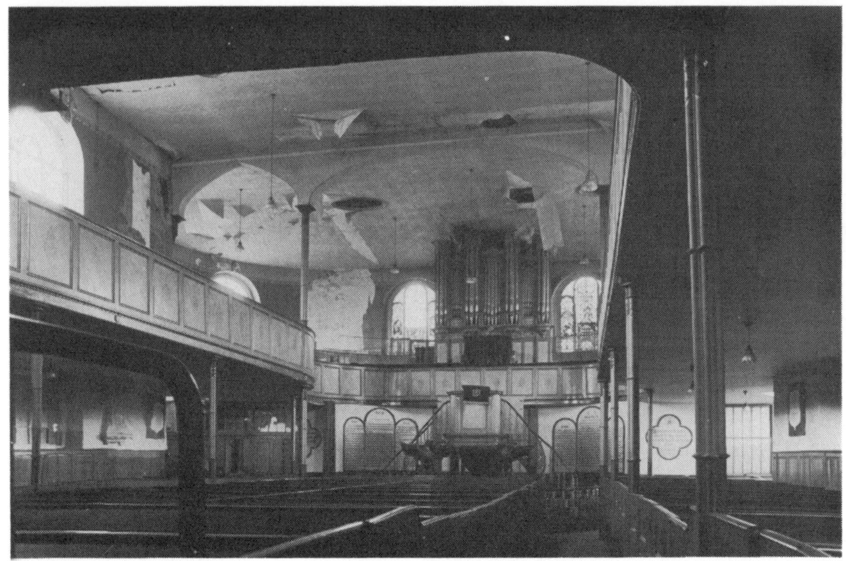

Fig 23a Worcester: Countess of Huntingdon's chapel, rebuilt 1804, extended to rear 1815 (photo: H Godwin Arnold)

freedom, confidence, and wealth, buildings could be far more elaborate and expensive. The vast difference between a Catholic church built for a wealthy patron, such as that designed by A W N Pugin for the Earl of Shrewsbury at Cheadle in Staffordshire (Fig 21), rich and glorious, and these early ones represents almost the whole length of scale between the two principles of church building from which we started.

Of the few fully developed Moravian settlements in England, those at Fairfield near Manchester and Fulneck near Pudsey in Yorkshire are the most complete. Fulneck, begun in 1742, was named after the early home of the church in Moravia. A long symmetrical frontage is composed of buildings of several dates. The earliest is the chapel which is in the centre, followed by two large pedimented brick houses near each end for the single brethren and single sisters but now occupied by boys' and girls' boarding schools. Other buildings were added between and nearby, including family houses and a widows' house, beside a workplace which was established for the manufacture of cloth.

The chapel has windows and doors dressed inside and out with classical surrounds in the style of James Gibbs's *Book of architecture* of 1732, which served as a pattern book for provincial architects and masons. The most distinctive feature of the chapel interior is the set of five elaborate swirling rococo plaster ceiling roses from which it may be assumed there

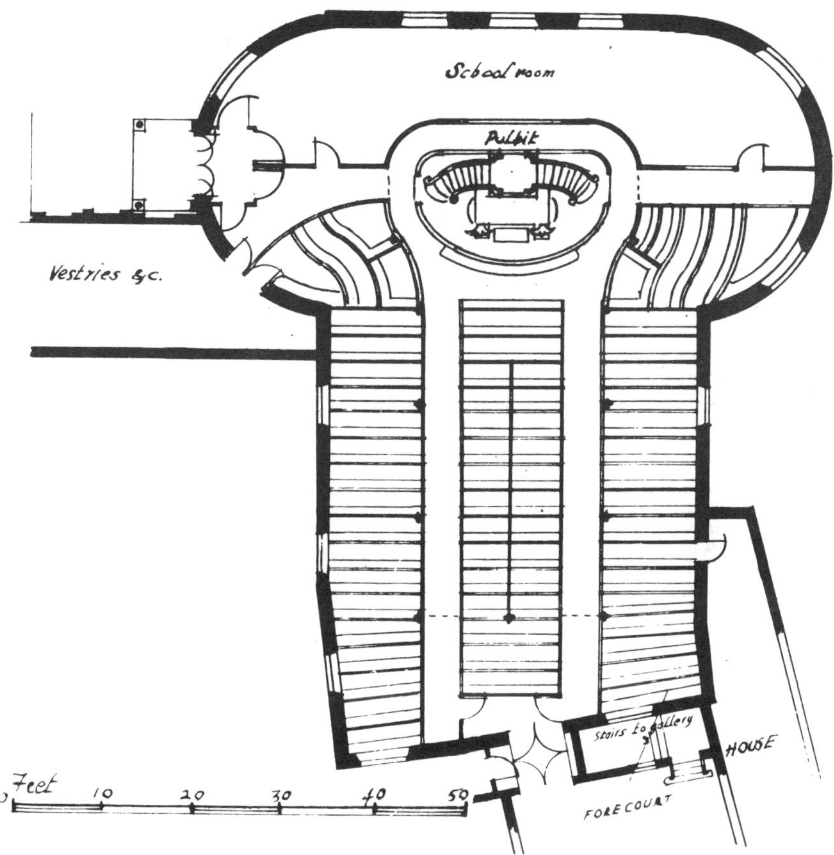

Fig 23b Worcester: Countess of Huntingdon's chapel (plan: H Godwin Arnold)

originally hung chandeliers. The pulpit is in the centre of one of the long sides, flanked by two pairs of tall windows, and the gallery runs round the remaining three sides (Fig 22).

John Wesley's connection with Count Zinzendorf and the settlement at Herrnhut has been mentioned. His companion George Whitefield had links with them in America. Selina, Countess of Huntingdon, who was Whitefield's supporter and patroness, had been an early follower of the Wesleys. She saw her mission as bringing Methodism to the aristocracy and the fashionable world, and established the body of Calvinistic Methodists known as 'The Countess of Huntingdon's Connexion'. In Bath she built a chapel, now closed, which has in front of it a neat little house for herself and her 'chaplains' in Georgian gothick style, with pointed sash windows and miniature battlements. Visiting the chapel, Horace Walpole wrote: 'The chapel is very neat, with true Gothic windows (yet I am not converted); but I was glad to see that luxury is creeping in upon them before persecution.... At the upper end is a broad *hautpas* of four steps, advancing in the middle: at each end of the broadest part are two of *my* eagles, with red cushions for the parson and clerk. Behind them rise three more steps, in the midst of which is a third eagle for pulpit. Scarlet armed chairs to all three. On either hand, a balcony for elect ladies. The rest of the congregation sit on forms.'

Another fine building of the same Connexion is that at Worcester (Fig 23), also now closed, and only saved from demolition after a long struggle. This also has a splendid pair of eagles as reading desks. The internal arrangement is very similar to that of the Bath chapel described by Walpole except that here the pulpit is more conventional but, for symmetry, is flanked by a pair of staircases. Between the pulpit and the pair of eagles is a small communion table, the whole group enclosed by an elliptical rail. On the walls alongside are panels with Creed and Commandments, the Lord's Prayer, and other texts from Epistles, Psalms, and the Old and New Testaments.

A list of denominations must have an end arbitrarily imposed, however fascinating it might be to explore the ways of Glassites, Sandemanians, Old Scots Independents, Bryanites, Agapemonites, Swedenborgians, Warrenite Methodists, the Scottish 'United Secession' church, or the 19th century religious history of a city such as Liverpool where even more can be found, with buildings changing readily from one denomination to the next. Such explorations must be left to others and we will close this survey with a denomination once influential, but now scarcely known, that of the Catholic Apostolic Church, sometimes called the 'Irvingites'. This developed in the 1830s around Edward Irving, minister of a Scots church in London from which he was eventually expelled for pentecostalist practices; his followers, including Henry Drummond and other wealthy persons, were persuaded of the prophetic appointment of latterday Apostles to rule the church until the second coming of Christ, which was considered imminent. A possibly deliberate failure to provide for the replacement of Apostles on whom ministerial ordination depended has left the church without officers or regular services though still with a few buildings of architectural interest. These were built for an elaborate ritual which even at its zenith the church must have had some difficulty in maintaining.

Henry Drummond, a member of a wealthy banking family, had bought an estate at Albury Park in Surrey in 1819. Here were held the first conferences for the study of prophecy and here the new Apostles of the church found a convenient centre for their work. After repairing the old parish church with the help of A W N Pugin, resiting the village, and

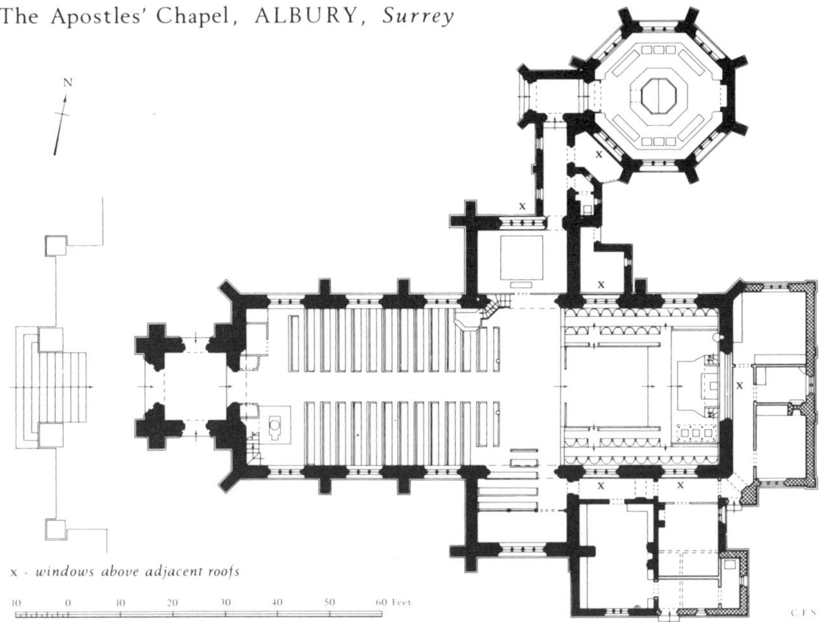

Fig 24 Albury, Surrey: Catholic Apostolic chapel, opened 1840 (plan: C F Stell, Crown copyright reserved)

building a new redbrick parish church to the designs of W MacIntosh Brookes, Drummond turned his attention to erecting the 'Apostles Chapel' (Fig 24) by the same architect, but with some of the fittings possibly designed by Pugin. The church is wide and cruciform but without aisles. There is a very small west gallery and the organ now occupies the north transept. Because of the width necessary for elaborate ceremonial, the choir is unusually spacious; the two side walls are lined with stalls of the pattern found in medieval cathedral choirs, 38 in number, and to the south of the altar is a set of three canopied thrones or sedilia. To the north is an octagonal 'chapter house' which served as a conference room for the Apostles. The chapel, though well maintained, is now closed and visitors are not encouraged. Ready access can, however, be gained to their former 'Central Church' by John Raphael Brandon, in Gordon Square, London, of 1854, now the University church. This magnificent Gothic building called for a staff of 64 to perform the elaborate ceremonies of the liturgy — an angel, six elders, six prophets, six evangelists, and seven deacons, acolytes, under-deacons, deaconesses, and lay-assistants. Vestments, lamps, tabernacles, stained glass, ornaments, were all on the same scale.

Fig 25 Goodshaw, Lancashire: Baptist chapel of late 18th century, refronted early 19th century, now in care of English Heritage (photo: NMR, Crown copyright reserved)

Fig 26 Manchester: First Church of Christ Scientist, Victoria Park, 1903, by Edgar Wood (photo: John Archer Collection)

Nowhere else in England at the time could such ceremonies be witnessed, not in the Roman Catholic church, still in the process of reorganizing after years of suppression, nor in the Church of England, where growing High Church practices were being countered by legal action such as the 'Purchas Judgement' of 1871.

The contrast between the Catholic Apostolic Church and the Society of Friends could not be greater; the mysteries of an incense-laden ritual and the quiet voice breaking the silence of a meeting seem poles apart, but both serve the same ultimate purpose. Modes of worship and places of worship vary immensely; some will attract, others may not speak to our condition, but for a variety which no Act of Uniformity could stifle we may indeed be truly thankful (Figs 25, 26).

2 Seekers, finders, and diggers

We saw in the previous chapter something of the richness and variety which exists in the architecture of the nonconformist churches. It remains now to seek, perhaps to find, certainly to dig.

Whether the object is to record a single building, our local 'Ebenezer', or to engage in a wider project, the first necessity is to locate the buildings that we intend to record. Locating and identifying chapels and meeting houses may call for considerable detective skill. Not all bodies of worshippers set out to proclaim their message or their presence from the rooftops: many of the older meeting houses are located on obscure sites and some of the smaller denominations still observe a reticence calculated to discourage any but the most persistent enquirer.

Preliminary work will generally require documentary research, particularly in the case of chapels which have passed to other uses. Ordnance Survey maps, local directories, denominational Year Books, and other published sources will all be a useful basis on which to start. To these may then be added, according to the nature of the project, the documentary material available in local history collections in libraries and County Record Offices. All this matter must be treated with circumspection for none of it, not least the printed material, will be found to be either infallible or complete.

Denominational lists, some of which go back to the mid 19th century or before, will be useful whether our interest is restricted to one denomination or covers the many which have been active in our area of study. Latest editions should be available in public libraries but for earlier copies recourse to college or denominational libraries may be necessary. It should be remembered that these are lists of local congregations, and generally give their dates of formation which need not coincide with the erection of any building. The principal lists which attempt to date individual chapels are those issued by the Moravians and Unitarians, together with the more recent returns of the Methodist Division of Property.

It is very hard to locate particular chapels from such lists alone. Full postal addresses are seldom given, obscure local names abound, and even nicknames which are known only to a favoured few. 'Providence' named on a Methodist preaching plan for the vast Devon parish of Hartland could never be identified without further assistance. Even in topographical directories such as *Kelly's* we may only be directed to a village or some ill-defined part of a large parish; here some dates are given, but confusion between the dates of formation of societies and of the erection of buildings frequently occurs. For further details local guidebooks and particularly the older town histories are useful; sometimes they include excellent accounts of all the places of worship within the town, even to specifying the cost of the building and the number of seats.

The earliest editions of the large-scale Ordnance Survey maps will be found particularly helpful in identifying the existence and allegiance of chapels in use a century ago. In villages and the countryside the 6in series is generally adequate, but for urban areas the 25in (1:2500) maps are preferable. Sometimes the building indicated by the lettering on the map is not at all clear, and denominational names have on occasion been found to be either wrong or misleading. For example, a Friends' meeting house which was temporarily in use as a Wesleyan chapel would be so named. The very large town plans at 1:500 scale are of especial value, where they exist. Some even show details of the layout of seating.

If the building is still standing but in an altered state, recognition may not be easy. The steeply-pitched roof of a former chapel can often be spotted from a distance above the surrounding houses; a house named 'Wesley Cottage' or 'Quakers Rest' may draw attention to its former use; and a street name such as Zion Place, Chapel Street, or Meeting House Lane may remain long after the congregation and their building have departed. Identification presents further difficulties where more than one chapel once stood in close proximity; the one sought may have gone and another hitherto unknown be then wrongly identified. Schools, halls, and even workshops can all easily be mistaken for former chapels and only experience will distinguish them where visual evidence is unsupported by documentary proof. By all means consult the neighbours or the oldest inhabitants, but remember that their memory may be uncertain and should always be checked against other sources.

A quest for chapels, exploring the physical setting of what has already been gleaned from written sources, inevitably prompts reflections on the changes which cause congregations to rise and fall. The seeker must be as sensitive to this historical dimension — the match of building to need, of certain forms of faith to their contemporary society — as to the physical impact of such changes on the building which he has tracked down. A strong constitution will be required to face with tact and diplomacy many of the alterations of successive congregations or of secular owners. Whether or not the changes are architectural improvements, which they seldom are, the searching and recording must go on before one more irreplaceable piece in the puzzle we are attempting to solve is swept away.

Even though we may have found the building for which we were looking and satisfied ourselves that no mistakes have been made in identification, much remains to be done. We will wish to record some aspects of the building now before us. The problems of doing so will be discussed in the next chapter. We will also need to discover more of its history and that of the congregation which worshipped there, or indeed which still does.

The manuscript records may be divided into two principal categories: those relating to the legal ownership and use of the building, and those covering the day-to-day affairs of the society meeting there. Most nonconformist buildings are trust property, the trustees being private persons or trust corporations who hold the property for such religious or charitable purposes as the trust deeds seek to lay down. The deeds refer to the site as much as to the building standing on it and so may be much older than an existing chapel. They will normally remain with the new owner after a change in use and will give valuable information about those members and others who have served on the trust. They may also make some statement about any doctrinal restrictions which had to be enforced, but which may, over the years, have been altered or forgotten.

Meeting houses for 'Protestants dissenting from the Church of England' were required by the 1689 Act of Toleration to be registered with the Quarter Sessions or the episcopal authorities, and such certificates of registration may remain with the trust deeds or other church papers. They are generally a good indication of the date from which the chapel was in use, but sometimes application was not made until local circumstances forced the congregation to conform. After 1837 registration for marriages was also possible and these certificates, too, may survive. Access to title deeds may be difficult, although owners are often willing to allow inspection by suitably accredited persons. Some early deeds have been deposited in County Record Offices and so are readily available, and in a few instances they have been printed as an appendix to a chapel history.

Minute books of various kinds should be looked for, and when found their deposit in record offices actively encouraged. These include trustees' minutes, the records of building committees, and the minutes of church meetings and of all the various societies which gather under the banner of a flourishing congregation. The minutes of larger organizations will illustrate the wider interests of local churches; the records of county associations, Methodist circuits, Friends' quarterly meetings, and many others may produce yet more valuable information. In all these, references to repairs and rebuilding, as well as matters of social concern, are to be discovered. More minutely, the detailed discussions, quarrels and divisions, hopes and achievements of congregations large or small may be found preserved in the crabbed hand of a beleaguered secretary or the biblical prose of a learned minister on the fading pages of the 'church book'.

Plans of chapels occasionally survive, ranging from a tiny outline of the site on the trust deeds to rolls of architect's drawings lying dirty and forgotten above a vestry cupboard. Relevant plans and correspondence may sometimes be found with the records of the estate from which the ground was acquired. Copies of plans relating to buildings which have been demolished may be sought in the files of the local planning authority.

Old photographs and drawings of chapels will often be discovered, some lovingly displayed in the vestry yet fading after years of continued exposure to the daylight, others with cracked glass in broken frames consigned to those piles of lumber in galleries, under pulpits, and in forgotten corners whence at last some new broom will sweep them into the furnace or off to the tip. Many illustrations were made as a record at a time when alterations were due to take place, or in the full pride of a newly-completed scheme. All are valuable chapters in the story we are trying to tell; seek them out and if possible have them copied before they perish. Some models of chapels also exist, and these may add further to our knowledge by including parts of the building outside the range of the photographer or the artist.

Look out for scrapbooks and other collections of ephemera from which, among the centenary brochures, old service papers, and newsletters, further forgotten facts — or pious fictions — may emerge. Collecting cards for subscribers to a building project may come to light or newspaper cuttings with reports of past celebrations — stone layings, chapel openings, and festivals of all kinds. This may lead to a more extensive search of files of newspapers or denominational magazines in which items of local news were sometimes reported in great detail.

All this assumes a readiness by church officers, ministers, secretaries, and others to allow free access to their premises and their records. Sometimes a chance call and brief explanation are all that is required. More often a letter and an appointment will be needed. Do not be surprised if it seems to be supposed that a brief glance around is good enough: few custodians of church property or records yet recognize the historical importance of their charge. It is up to those who do to educate the rest as politely but as firmly as possible. Be prepared for the occasional refusal of an innocent request, for not all officers are alike, but with time and patience we may hope to achieve our goal

3 A permanent record

Discovery of the historical background, the names of architect and builder, the dates and cost of building and alterations, and other matters, may still leave us without a clear picture of the building in which we are interested. The aim, if it is our intention to produce a record which will be of permanent value even after conversion or demolition has taken its toll, must be to complete the picture by drawings, sketches, photographs, and written notes. Succeeding generations will want to know where the chapel stood, its size and materials, the kind and quality of the fittings, and where they were placed. Our record will serve as a basis of comparison with work in other localities, periods, or denominations. It will be of value to historians if we are careful to make sure that facts and those theories of development which will certainly occur to us as we work are clearly distinguished in our record. No particular expertise is required beyond a willingness to take the trouble to be accurate, but it would be unwise to undertake more than our time or ability justifies. Isometric projections or photographs of large dimly-lit interiors may have to be left to more expert hands, but there is much that the amateur can do to prevent many a worthy building from passing away for ever unrecorded. It is to the enthusiastic amateur, therefore, standing in an unfamiliar building with clipboard and measuring rod in hand, that these notes are particularly addressed.

It is easy for the amateur, and sometimes for the professional as well, when faced with a building of unusual interest or complexity, to be discouraged by the apparent size of the task. Even in a simple building it is essential to understand that no record, however full, can cover every possible feature. The essential skill is to choose between what is basic and must therefore be set down precisely and what is secondary and may be treated in outline. In either case the result must be sufficiently accurate for others to use with confidence, and the limitations of the record (as, for example, where a plan is paced rather than measured or where selected inscriptions only are transcribed) should be made clear. To devote our time to the minute description of mouldings or organ cases, for example, while omitting to record their general setting would be unwise unless they happen to be our primary object. Our ambition should be rather to finish the survey at a modest level than to risk failure by our clear inability to record everything within sight.

The scale at which we draw the survey is open to choice and depends on our skill and the amount of detail we wish to show. A scale of 1:200 (sixteenth of an inch to one foot) is adequate for many purposes and yields a useful layout plan, particularly if the principal internal dimensions are noted on the drawing itself. It is convenient for copying and storing as the plan will generally fit on an A4 sheet and it avoids the temptation to include minute detail, such as window mouldings, which are better shown in a separate sketch. A larger scale of 1:100 or even 1:50 (eighth or quarter inch to one foot) may suit the more skilful draughtsman or special requirements but will demand extra care in the initial survey.

A typical record which would not be over-ambitious but which would be of permanent value might comprise the following:

1 The location by present name, original denomination, county, town, or civil parish, and an accurate six-figure reference to the National Grid.
2 A measured plan of the building including internal features, with annotations of all points of interest.
3 A plan of the site, where this is of appreciable extent, possibly paced rather than measured, drawn to an approximate scale of 1:500 to show boundary walls and the names of adjacent roads and other properties; both this and the previous plan to include a drawn scale and compass point.
4 A set of photographs to include all the outer walls and the general setting of the building, remembering that the back elevation, so seldom photographed, may be as important as the front; interior photographs are particularly necessary, even though calling for greater skill, as are photographs of any special decorative features or fittings.

Before embarking on such a survey some essential preparations must be made. The necessity for prior permission has already been stressed, and it is important to be able to give some indication of the time you may need to spend within the building. Large-scale maps will be helpful in providing the basis for a site plan and in giving a general idea of the outline of the building. An existing plan of the chapel may be available which could save further time, but its accuracy should never be assumed. Plans made for alterations or repairs, for drainage, or for other services, may have been adequate for their purpose but as records their value is limited.

The equipment needed for the kind of survey proposed is to some extent a matter of personal choice, but the following are suggested:

1 A clip-board and a pad of stout paper — squared paper may be found helpful at first to obtain correct proportions and to avoid too much rubbing out — together with a good supply of pencils of a suitable grade, not too hard.
2 Measuring tapes, including a long tape of up to 100ft for overall measurements and a short steel tape of up to 12ft for the smaller details. Some tapes have a hook to anchor the end at a suitable corner, but a knife or steel skewer will be found useful when no other assistance is to be had. A folding rod is also serviceable, particularly for vertical measurements, but greater heights call for some ingenuity in the use

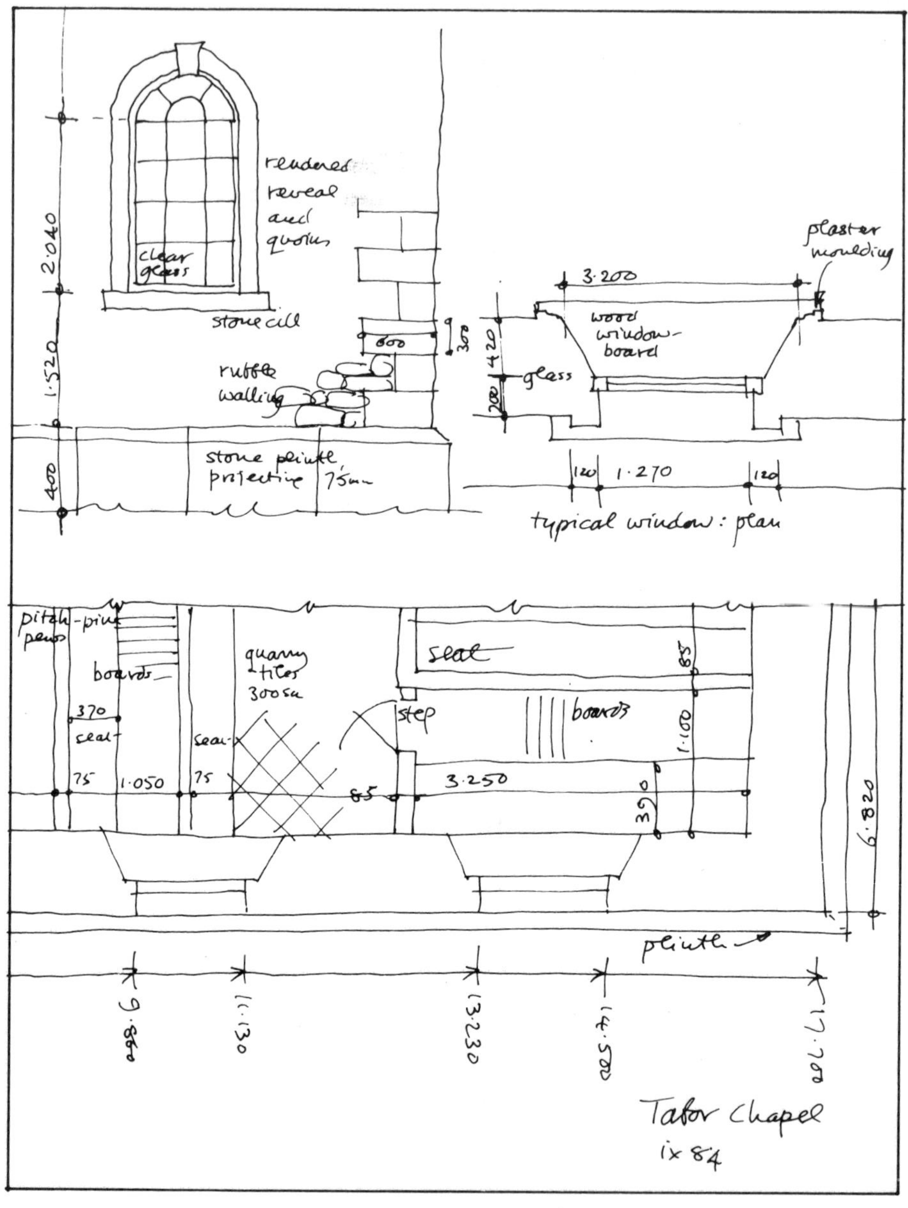

Fig 27 Extract from site survey sheet, showing use of running dimensions, elevation sketch, and typical annotations

of garden canes, chimney-sweeps' rods, etc; if absolute accuracy is not necessary, one of the optical measuring devices might be useful.

3 For photographs a 35mm single-lens reflex camera is most suitable, with a wide-angle lens of 35mm or 28mm focal length essential for interiors. Good record photographs are the result of experience rather than sophisticated equipment, and with suitable film and a wide aperture even interiors may be tackled without the use of a tripod or flash. Although slides will be found useful when giving talks, black and white prints are still preferable for record purposes. These are preferred by the National Monuments Record, to whose collections additions are always welcome. Colour prints may be desirable at times, but they are not usually as precise in detail and their permanence is still in question.

Before taking any measurements it is as well to spend a little time getting the feel of the building. Begin work by preparing a careful sketch plan on which to set down the dimensions and notes (Fig 27). This should be large enough to allow these to be inserted without undue overcrowding. The main block of a building is often most easily surveyed externally by running measure: fix the tape at one corner (or get an assistant to hold one end), preferably above the level of the lower window sills, and read off the measurements of the opening or other features in sequence. Running dimensions avoid cumulative error and make for easier and more accurate drawing out later. Within this framework individual features may be added by separate measurement; wall thicknesses can be obtained easily at window openings by measuring from inner and outer faces of the wall to the line of the glass. Remember that not all walls in a building will be of the same thickness, particularly those of porches and other minor appendages. Internal measurements should be taken by running measurement whenever possible to include at least the outline of the seating and other principal fittings. Staircases need not be fully measured so long as the number of risers has been correctly noted and the arrangement at corners and landings properly sketched. The more intricate details of door architraves should generally be omitted and such features as fireplace recesses and larger items of furniture, such as organs, may be reduced to a simple outline. Where it is not possible to assume that walls are at right-angles, diagonal measurements between opposite corners should be taken to give an accurate triangulation from which the angles can be found. Drawn sections or elevations can be helpful in some instances, but the time necessary to complete them must be weighed against that available for recording the principal features or contents of the building. These include the recording of date stones, foundation stones, memorials, and fittings of all kinds including window glass, as well as any evidence that may appear of alterations to the main fabric.

Fig 28 Nonconformist burial grounds may be affected by the 'thinning' or complete clearance of memorials: some of the gravestones visible in this photograph (Underbank chapel, Stannington, West Yorkshire, built 1742–43) are no longer there (photo: C F Stell)

For a general site plan it may be sufficient to pace out the ground, bearing in mind that, unless carefully checked, one's paces may vary according to the haste in which the work is carried out. The site plan should cover the extent of the ground and of any graveyard attached, together with any buildings and pathways including special monuments or other features. Any old openings which may have been blocked in the outer or surrounding walls should be noted. The dates of the earliest and latest monuments should be recorded; if a more detailed record of graveyard monuments is desired, it must be done with the greatest care (Figs 28, 29).

In drawing out from the survey (Fig 30), remember that it is most satisfactory to do this as soon as possible while all remains fresh in one's mind. Always aim at a neat and tidy presentation, which will encourage confidence in its accuracy and help to ensure its preservation as an important record (Fig 31). In the absence of a drawing board and T-square, a pad of tracing paper above a square grid underlay may be used, but these two basic pieces of equipment will be found essential to any serious draughtsmanship, together with an adjustable set-square and a set

GRAVE MEMORIAL RECORDING FORM

	CEMETERY or GRAVEYARD		
	DEDICATION or DENOMINATION		
1	NAT. GRID REF.		
2	DATE of RECORD		
3	NAME of RECORDER or GROUP		
4	MEMORIAL No. and LETTER		
5	No. of COMPONENTS		
6	ASSOCIATED FORM LETTERS		
7	Memorial type: 1. flat 2. head 3. tomb 4. foot 5. other		
8	MATERIAL and GEOLOGY		
9	STONE MASON or UNDERTAKER		
10	Which faces are inscribed? – compass points		
11	No. of people commemorated		
12	TECHNIQUE of INSCRIPTION		
13	Condition of monument: 1. sound, in situ 2. sound displaced 3 leaning or falling apart 4. collapsed 5. overgrown		
14	Condition of inscription: 1. mint 2. clear but worn 3. mainly decipherable 4. traces 5. illegible or destroyed		
15	DIMENSIONS	Height	
16	(in mms.)	Width	
17		Thickness	
18	PHOTOGRAPH NEGATIVE No.		
19	ORIENTATION	N 1, 2, 3 E, 4, 5 S, 6, W 7, 8	which way stone faces

Fig 29 The CBA produces this form for the recording of graveyard memorials; for guidance on the use of the form, and on the recording of graveyards generally, consult J. Jones 1984

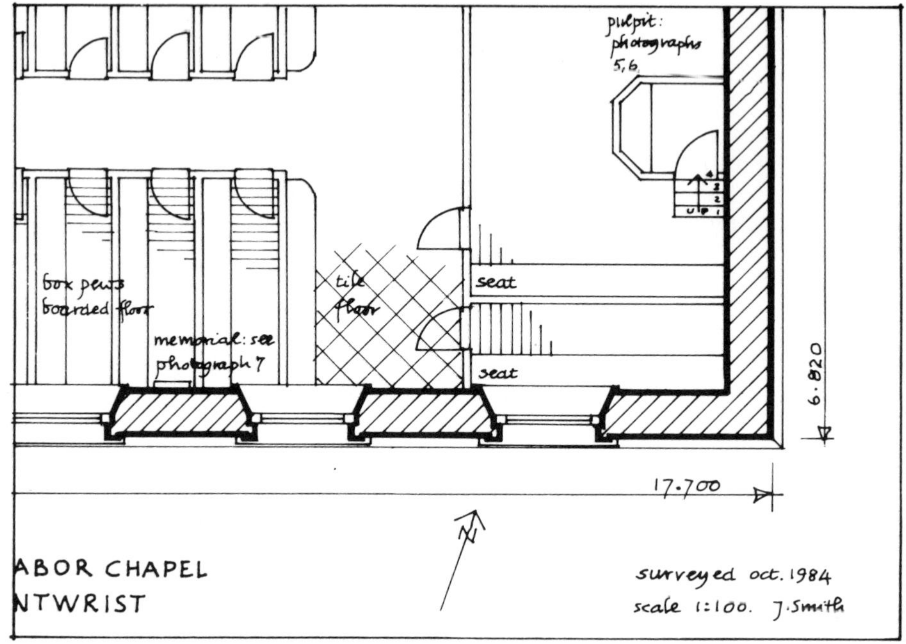

Fig 30 Extract from finished drawing

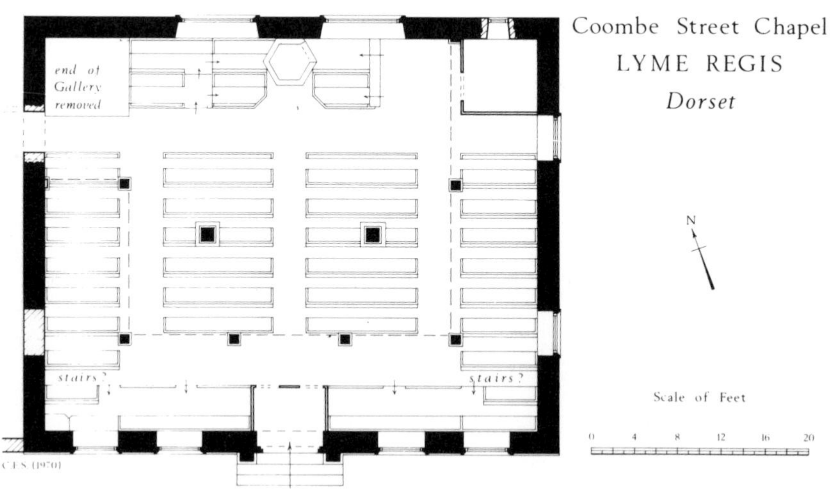

Fig 31 A plan ready for publication. Lyme Regis, Dorset: Coombe Street chapel, 1746 (plan: C F Stell, Crown copyright reserved)

of architect's scales, as well as Indian ink drawing pens with nibs of two or three different thicknesses. For most purposes a standard A4 sheet of paper will be large enough at the scales suggested, though A3 may be required; both sizes are suitable for photocopying by most of the machines which are becoming publicly available.

The scale to which plans are drawn and the dimensions used, whether imperial or metric, are very much a matter of personal choice, but do not forget that a knowledge of the units of measurement employed by the original builders may have an important bearing on an understanding of their intentions and on an explanation of the extent of subsequent changes. Style of presentation is also very much a personal matter, but look at published plans in the leading archaeological periodicals where good and indifferent examples can easily be distinguished. A bold outline in ink with different periods indicated by line hatching of various forms will probably be found best and may be coloured later if required (though not if the drawing is intended for publication). Much solid black infilling may present difficulties unless the paper is sufficiently stout to prevent distortion. Plans at more than one level are seldom needed, though this will depend on the object of the exercise and the time available. All drawings should have a clearly drawn scale (in both imperial and metric units) and a north point, with the name of the building, the date recorded, and the name of the person responsible. It may also be useful to include the main internal measurements for ease of reference.

The form of record suggested, though capable of infinite variations to suit individual tastes, may thus comprise an A4 sheet showing the floor plan and another with the site plan, possibly a photocopy of the old 1:500 OS town plan, and a selection of photographs mounted on sheets of matching size. This is a manageable form of record, easily made, stored, copied, posted, and displayed. It can be bound in a loose-leaf folder, and for occasional displays the sheets can be mounted on a large board. These considerations of reproduction, transmission, and display are all-important if the work is to be made available to a wider public, even in a limited way. The cost of recording a chapel or meeting house is not great once the basic equipment has been acquired, even though transport, photography, and photocopying (and an appropriate contribution to church funds) should all be taken into consideration.

As you cover the ground, as you record more of the chapels in your neighbourhood or of your selected denomination, so will the usefulness of the work increase. Thus in the end you will deal not only with the oldest and the smartest but also with the most ordinary chapels and all that lie between; by that time you will have made the acquaintance of people doing the same thing elsewhere. At this stage a whole host of ideas flows, projects for future study based on days spent in cold chapels and evenings deciphering notes over a drawing board. They include comparisons of one

Fig 32a Halifax, West Yorkshire: Square Chapel, 1772 (photo: NMR, Crown copyright reserved)

Fig 32b Bristol, New Room, 1739/48 (photo: NMR, Crown copyright reserved)

district with another, one denomination or period with another, chronology of plan type, design standards, architects' and builders' costs, local and imported materials, and the vernacular building styles; they present unlimited opportunities and unending pleasure.

4 Preservation of the record

Apart from pleasant memories, the only result to show for the time, effort, and money spent on recording a building might easily be a file of miscellaneous papers, notes, plans, and photographs. It makes sense therefore to compile the notes and surveys in such a way that other people may find them helpful, and better still to place them where they may be permanently accessible to a wider public. Even if your record is published, it will be possible to include only a fraction of the material, so the clarity and the assembling of the original record remain of prime importance.

It is fatally easy to fall into the habit of using scrappy bits of paper for notes, so ensure that you use a standard presentation right from the start. Date all notes and surveys, write titles on slides and photographs, and index negatives.

It can be difficult to part with something that has been a source of such great personal interest as the papers relating to a survey, but if your work is to have any lasting significance the record must be made available to other people. This means finding a secure home which will ensure the preservation of your record for the foreseeable future in good conditions, and which will be accessible to future researchers whose interests may embrace architecture, denominational history, liturgy, sociology, and much more.

County Record Offices meet all these requirements; indeed, probably no other institutions can do so in quite the same way. Museums are seldom suitable repositories and too often a local museum may not outlast the enthusiastic local historians who first set it up. Specialist private libraries belonging to relevant societies and institutions often appeciate *copies* rather than original material, since they can not always offer the same accessibility as a Record Office.

So when you have decided that your contribution to the survey is complete, arrange the material in files as far as possible, and add an explanatory note as to its compilation and authorship. Make it clear that information in it may be freely used, or note any restrictions. Then approach the local Record Office, the address of which will be listed in the telephone directory or obtainable from your local reference library, and explain what you have to deposit. The Record Office will include it in its own listings and indexes, but it would also be very helpful if you were to inform any appropriate learned society so that it could note the deposit in its journal or newsletter.

It remains an irresistible temptation to rush into print, despite the effects of inflation on printing costs, but do first consider carefully whether the likely readership would be satisfied by photocopies of a neatly typed script on A4 sheets. It costs no more than £5 (at current prices) to reproduce at least 50 sheets of A4 paper, which is a modest sum for a great deal of information. If a wider publication still seems worthwhile, however, there are two possibilities. Either a booklet can be published privately, which will depend upon sales to cover costs, or a paper can be offered to the editor of some appropriate learned society's journal. If your offer is accepted, the costs will be wholly or largely borne by the society. A third choice could be a commercial publishing house, but this is unrealistic for the sort of material envisaged.

Whichever method is followed, it is probable that no more than a part of the material collected can be published; but remember too that this need not be too great a disadvantage if the survey can be consulted in a Record Office. It means, however, that what is printed should serve not only to interpret the facts as seen by the compiler but to point the way to the permanent record on which future discussion will increasingly rely.

A paper in a journal has many attractions: the financial implications are minimal and the readership assured. But in today's financial climate many journals can only include illustrations if donations are made, and there is also the constraint of editorial approval. Editors might resist a continuing series of articles on different chapels. If your article cannot be accepted it is still well worth seeking to include a brief note about the survey and where it can be consulted. Even if it is published, it is important to give these details. Many journals have small circulations, but they are distributed widely and their contents are indexed.

Private publication can mean almost anything, from a substantial book to a few photocopied sheets stapled together; with care, a serviceable booklet with card covers and illustrations can be produced from this simple material. In recent years photocopying machines have become very versatile and economic for long runs, or more traditional forms of duplication may be used; if stencils can be typed and run off, and the pages stapled by volunteers, this is a cheap and effective method. Illustrations may need to be produced on electronic stencils, and these are expensive.

Most towns and some colleges have jobbing printers who will offer offset litho facilities. This is a superior method but more costly.

Producing a little booklet by your own efforts is very satisfying, but it may need to be subsidized, for sales seldom meet expectations. Do not forget the obligation to give complimentary copies to people who have provided help. It might be a starting point to consider a print run of 100 copies but do set the price so that you will recover costs on no more than half the number printed.

5 The legislation relating to nonconformist places of worship

In 1913 Archbishop Davidson secured for the Anglican Church the principle of the 'ecclesiastical exemption' from the effects of ancient monuments legislation in return for the promised resuscitation of the faculty system, and by the early 1920s such a system of protection came effectively into force. For it legally to be done, any repair, rebuilding, replacement, or reconstruction of an Anglican church and the introduction of any new furnishings or the permanent or temporary removal of any existing furnishings now require a licence or 'faculty' from the Chancellor of the diocese, though certain relatively unimportant changes can be authorized by Archdeacon's certificate.

The principle of the ecclesiastical exemption was extended to nonconformist places of worship in use, even though there is nothing in the structure of these denominations to compare with the faculty system. The Methodists, for example, have a Division of Property in Manchester that is able to provide advice on problems relating to the care and maintenance of its buildings, but final responsibility rests with the trustees. The United Reformed Church, while it has a central administration, has no department concerned specifically with church buildings.

Listed nonconformist places of worship (including college or school chapels) in use for ecclesiastical purposes, then, are in general exempt from listed building controls but not from planning controls. Planning permission is needed where any 'development', as that word has been broadly defined in successive Town and Country Planning Acts, is involved. The word covers not only building works 'in, on, over, or under' land (which will, of course, cover extensions and new buildings in the curtilage of the property), but also, for example, changes of use and significant modifications to the external appearance of a building including changes in roof coverings.

The total demolition of a listed nonconformist chapel requires Listed Building Consent, as does the total demolition of a similar unlisted building in a conservation area. But the part demolition, alteration, or extension of a listed chapel will not require Listed Building Consent (though it might require planning permission) where its use for ecclesiastical purposes will continue during the work or be only temporarily interrupted while the work is being carried out. (A listed manse, incidentally, is treated as not being an ecclesiastical building and will be subject to both planning controls and listed building controls in the normal way.)

The demolition, alteration (whether internal or external), or extension of a listed nonconformist chapel or meeting house not in ecclesiastical use will require Listed Building Consent. A change of use for such a building will not require Listed Building Consent but, as a matter of 'development', will require planning permission.

It should be noted, finally, that the listing of a building includes all other buildings within the curtilage of that building, whether or not they are specifically mentioned in the list, and that the word 'building' is defined sufficiently widely to cover churchyard monuments and tombstones which can therefore come within listed building controls.

Bibliography

The numerous works already in print which relate to nonconformist history are generally concerned with the origins and development of denominational characteristics, the lives of their principal protagonists, and the fortunes of their followers. Many histories of individual congregations or groups contain occasional references to the buildings occupied for worship, but relatively few include critical comment or analysis. The following lists, while not attempting to be exhaustive, include the principal general works and a selection of those of a more local nature.

I General

Arnold, H G, 1960 Early meeting-houses, *Trans Ancient Monuments Soc*, n ser, **8**, 89–139

Barton, D, 1975 *Discovering chapels and meeting houses*

Betjeman, J, 1940 Nonconformist architecture, *Architect Rev*, **88**, 160–74

Binfield, C, 1977 *So down to prayers: studies in English Nonconformity 1780–1920*

Binney, M, & Burman, P, 1977 *Chapels and churches: who cares?*

Briggs, M S, 1946 *Puritan architecture and its future*

Dolbey, G W, 1964 *The architectural expression of Methodism: the first hundred years*

Drummond, A L, 1934 *The church architecture of Protestantism*

——, 1938 The architectural interest of the English meeting house, *J Roy Inst Brit Architect*, August 15, 909–17

Evans, G E, 1897 *Vestiges of protestant dissent*

Jones, J, 1984 *How to record graveyards*, 3 edn

Jones, R P, 1914 *Nonconformist church architecture*

Kelly's Directory, county ser (London, various dates)

Lidbetter, H, 1946 Quaker meeting houses, 1670–1850, *Architect Rev*, **99**, 99–116

——, 1961 *The Friends meeting house*

Lindley, K, 1969 *Chapels and meeting houses*

Little, B, 1966 *Catholic churches since 1623*

Pevsner, Sir Nikolaus (ed), from 1951 *The buildings of England*

Stell, C F, in press *An inventory of Nonconformist chapels and meeting houses in central England*, Royal Commission on Historical Monuments (England)

Material for further volumes to cover the whole of England is awaiting publication

——, 1973–7 Our architectural heritage, *J United Reformed Church Hist Soc*, **1**, 158–73

——, 1976 *Architects of dissent: some Nonconformist patrons and their architects*, Friends of Dr Williams's Library, London

Thomas, J, 1976 Nonconformist architecture in Britain: a bibliography, *Research Bulletin, Institute for the Study of Worship and Religious Architecture*, 74–80

Twinn, K, *et al*, 1973 *Nonconformist congregations in Great Britain: a list of histories and other material in Dr Williams's Library*

Victoria County History of the Counties of England

II Regional and local studies

Allen, N V, 1974 *Churches and chapels of Exmoor*
Bielby, A R, 1978 *Churches and chapels of Kirklees*
Binfield, C, 1984 *Pastors and people: the biography of a Baptist church, Queens Road, Coventry*
Blake, S T, 1979 *Cheltenham's churches and chapels, AD 773–1883*
Brockett, A, 1962 *Nonconformity in Exeter, 1650–1875*
Butler, D M, 1978 *Quaker meeting houses of the Lake Counties*
Chambers, R F, continued by Oliver, R W, 1952–68 *The Strict Baptist chapels of England*, five vols covering southern and midland counties only
Clack, P A G, & Pattinson, K E, 1978 *Weardale chapels*
Cox, B G, 1982 *Chapels and meeting houses in the Vale of Evesham*
Dawson, D, 1982 Archaeology and the churches of Bristol, Abbots Leigh and Whitchurch, 1540–1850, *Bristol Avon Archaeol*, **1**, 28–44
Jones, A, 1984 *Welsh chapels*, Nat Mus Wales
Leary, W, 1969 *Methodism in the City of Lincoln, from its origin in the eighteenth century to the present day*
Mudie-Smith, R, 1904 *The religious life of London*
Nightingale, B, 1890–3 *Lancashire Nonconformity*, 6 vols
Powell, K, 1980 *The fall of Zion: northern chapel architecture and its future*
Probert, J C C, 1966 *The architecture of Cornish Methodism*
Seals, W F, 1974 *Methodism in the Otley Circuit, 1744–1974*
Spittal, J, & Dawson, D, 1983 *The Kingswood chapels survey*
Thorne, R F S, 1975 The last Bible Christians, their church in Devon, 1907, *Trans Devonshire Ass*, **107**, 47–75
——, 1983 *Methodism in Devon: a handlist of chapels and their records*, Devon Rec Off, Handlist 2
White, W M, 1971 *Six Weeks Meeting 1671–1971, three hundred years of Quaker responsibility*